Incredible Birds

John Townsend

www.raintreepublishers.co.uk
Visit our website to find out more information about **Raintree** books.

To order:
☎ Phone 44 (0) 1865 888113
📄 Send a fax to 44 (0) 1865 314091
💻 Visit the Raintree Bookshop at **www.raintreepublishers.co.uk** to browse our catalogue and order online.

First published in Great Britain by Raintree Publishers, Halley Court, Jordan Hill, Oxford, OX2 8EJ, part of Harcourt Education Ltd.
Raintree is a registered trademark of Harcourt Education Ltd.

© Harcourt Education Ltd 2005
First published in paperback in 2005.
The moral right of the proprietor has been asserted.

Produced for Raintree Publishers by Discovery Books Ltd
Editorial: Louise Galpine, Elisabeth Taylor, Charlotte Guillain, and Diyan Leake
Expert reader: Jill Bailey
Design: Victoria Bevan, Keith Williams (sprout.uk.com Limited), and Michelle Lisseter
Picture Research: Maria Joannou
Production: Duncan Gilbert and Jonathan Smith
Printed and bound in China by South China Printing Company
Originated by Repro Multi Warna

ISBN 1 844 43454 0 (hardback)
09 08 07 06 05
10 9 8 7 6 5 4 3 2 1

ISBN 1 844 43474 5 (paperback)
09 08 07 06 05
10 9 8 7 6 5 4 3 2 1

British Library Cataloguing in Publication Data
Townsend, John
Incredible Birds. – (Freestyle express. Incredible creatures)
598
A full catalogue record for this book is available from the British Library.

This levelled text is a version of Freestyle: Incredible creatures: Incredible birds.

Photo acknowledgements
The publisher would like to thank the following for permission to reproduce photographs: 2000 Dreamworks p. 51 (Pathe and Aardman); ANT Photography p. 6; Ardea p. 23 right (Hans D. Dossenbach); Corbis pp. 6–7, 18 (James L. Amos), 24 top, 34–5, 40 right (Frank W. Lane; Frank Lane Picture Agency), 47 right (Eric and David Hosking), 49 left, 49 right; FLPA pp. 4, 5 middle, 7, 8–9, 13, 14, 19 (Sunset), 20 left, 20 right, 23 left, 24 bottom, 25, 28 left, 28 right, 29, 31 top, 31 bottom, 32 left, 32 right, 33, 34, 35 (F. Polking), 36–7, 37, 38 right, 39, 40 left, 41, 42, 44, 46, 47 left, 48, 50; Naturepl pp. 5 top, 9, 17 (Dave Watts), 27 (Tony Heald); NHPA pp. 5 bottom (Paal Hermansen), 10 left, 10–11, 11 right, 14–15, 15, 16, 18–19, 21, 22, 26–7, 26, 30, 36 left, 38 left, 42–3 (Paal Hermansen), 44–5, 45, 50–1; Oxford Scientific Films pp. 8, 12 right, 16–17; Photodisc pp. 4–5, 12 left

Cover photograph of a bald eagle reproduced with permission of Steve Bloom

The Publishers would like to thank Jon Pearce for his assistance in the preparation of this book.

Every effort has been made to contact copyright holders of any material reproduced in this book. Any omissions will be rectified in subsequent printings if notice is given to the Publishers.

Contents

Any words appearing in the text in bold, **like this**, are explained in the Glossary. You can also look out for some of them in the 'Wild words' bank at the bottom of each page.

The world of birds

Would you believe it?

The South American bellbird is the loudest bird in the world. Its clanging sound can be heard several kilometres away.

What if you could fly?

What are birds?

Birds are the only animals that have feathers and beaks. They probably **evolved** from **reptiles** millions of years ago. As birds evolved, they grew wings instead of front legs.

▶ The bearded vulture (right) has one of the widest **wingspans** of any bird. At 3 metres, it is as long as a small car.

Warm-blooded

Reptiles are cold-blooded. Although birds are related to reptiles, they are warm-blooded. This means that their body temperature stays the same, no matter what the weather. They need to eat to keep warm. When people put out seeds and nuts in winter this helps birds to keep out the cold.

▶ The largest bird in the world is the ostrich. It cannot fly, but it runs very fast.

Find out later...

...which bird flies fastest.

...which bird kills snakes.

...why some crows watch traffic lights.

reptile cold-blooded animal with scales, such as a snake or lizard

Meet the family

All birds have feathers and everything that has feathers is a bird. There are about 9000 **species** of birds.

Why feathers?

Feathers keep air flowing around the bird's wings. This makes it fly and helps it to balance. Feathers weigh very little because they are hollow.

The colours and markings of feathers are important for **camouflage**. Some males have bright feathers to attract a female when they are looking for a **mate**.

Fancy feathers

The male ribbon-tailed astrapia has long tail feathers that look like white ribbons. He **displays** his beautiful tail to attract a mate.

Keeping warm

Soft, fluffy feathers help keep birds warm, even in freezing places like the Arctic. The whistling swan (below), from North America, may have as many as 25,000 feathers in winter. It loses many of these when it **moults** in summer.

Hard to see

The woodcock nests on the ground in woods. Its brown, speckled feathers are a good camouflage. It is hard to spot the female sitting on her nest.

▼ The oil in this swan's feathers makes it **waterproof**.

moult lose feathers before growing new ones

Fastest fliers

The fastest fliers all live on water. A mallard duck flies at 64 kilometres (40 miles) per hour. It wouldn't win a race against the eider duck (below) which can reach 75 kilometres (47 miles) per hour.

Flying birds

Inside birds' hollow bones are criss-crossing little bars of bone. These give them extra strength. Birds' beaks are also very light. They do not have teeth or jawbones adding to their weight. Even a large bird, like the snowy owl, weighs less than 3 kilograms (6 pounds). That weighs the same as three bags of flour. Much of its size is made up of fluffy feathers.

High fliers

Bar-headed geese **breed** in Tibet. They then fly over the Himalayas to India. They have to fly over 6000 metres (3.7 miles) high to get over these huge mountains.

Other birds, such as cranes, also fly over mountains. Godwits and curlews have been seen from Mount Everest in the Himalayas at 7000 metres (4.3 miles).

▼ Sandhill cranes fly high over Alaska. Sometimes some are found as far away as Ireland.

Fastest sprinters

The peregrine falcon (above) is the fastest **bird of prey** and can dive at speeds of up to 320 kilometres (200 miles) per hour. That is as fast as a Formula One racing car.

---

breed to produce young

King of the birds

The male peacock looks very beautiful when he opens out his huge, fan-shaped tail of feathers. He does this to attract a **mate**.

Flap and flutter

Some birds hardly fly at all. They only go short distances to **roost** in trees or to escape **predators**.

Pheasants, chickens, and turkeys have large bodies and small wings. They cannot fly for very long at a time. Some water birds, such as moorhens, keep safe by hiding in reeds. They do not often fly.

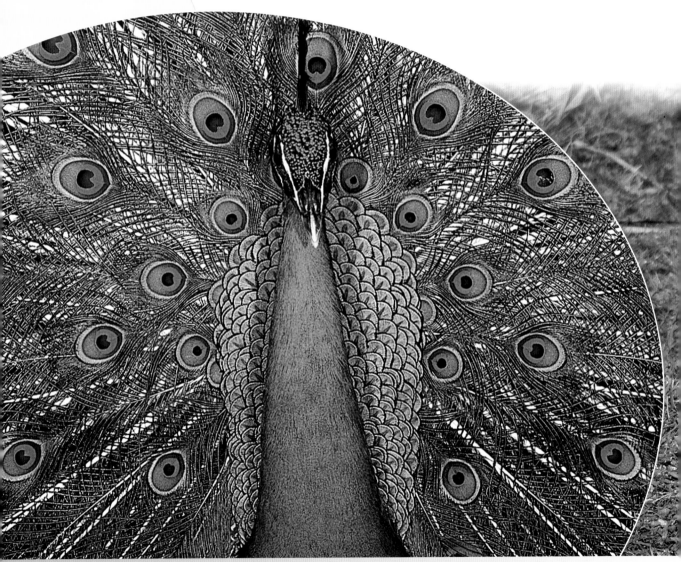

roost settle down to sleep

Flightless and extinct

The dodo was a **flightless** bird that lived on the island of Mauritius. Dutch people moved there in the 1500s. It was easy for them to hunt the flightless dodo for food. Within a hundred years it had become **extinct**.

In New Zealand the flightless takahe was easily hunted by **settlers** and their dogs. Many thought it had become extinct. But in 1948 a few takahe were discovered surviving in the mountains. It is still **endangered**.

Wild chickens

The chickens that are farmed for eggs and meat were first **bred** from a wild bird, the red jungle fowl. This probably happened about 5000 years ago.

▲ The New Zealand takahe cannot fly.

extinct died out, never to return

Runners

Some **flightless** birds are able to run away from **predators**. The emu has strong legs and can run at 64 kilometres (40 miles) an hour. It can swim too.

The cassowary runs at its enemy and attacks with a vicious kick. It looks quite scary too – with its horned head, blue neck, and huge claws.

Long-distance walker

Australia's largest bird, the emu, follows rainclouds in search of water. It can walk over 450 kilometres (300 miles) to find some.

▲ The cassowary makes a deep, booming call when it attacks.

predator animal that hunts and eats other animals

Ostriches

The huge ostrich lives on the grass plains of Africa. It can kill with a kick and has even killed humans in this way.

Ostriches can run without stopping for 15 to 20 minutes. They may travel up to 24 kilometres (15 miles). They live mostly on seeds and plants but sometimes eat insects and small animals. Like chickens, ostriches scratch the ground to get at their food.

Kiwis

The kiwi has tiny wings and cannot fly. It has a very good sense of smell, which helps it sniff out food in the soil.

▶ Kiwis are not often seen as they come out at night.

Great auks

Great auks used to nest on rocky islands in the north Atlantic. Sailors and fishermen hunted them. They used their meat to catch fish. Due to this, these birds became **extinct** in 1844.

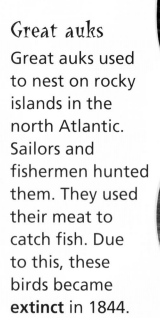

Swimmers

On land, penguins walk slowly and cannot fly. But they can swim as well as fish in the sea. Their wings act like flippers and they appear to fly through the water. They can leap from the sea at speed to land on the ice above.

Penguin feathers sit very close together. They are made for warmth, not for flight. They are like a woolly, **waterproof** coat, full of oil. They keep penguins warm in the coldest of seas.

　waterproof does not let in water

There are seventeen **species** of penguin, all of which live in cold seas in the Southern **Hemisphere**. They swim together in groups. This keeps them safer from **predators** like leopard seals and killer whales.

Emperor penguins are the largest penguins. They can stay under the freezing water for 12 minutes looking for fish. They may swim up to 400 kilometres (250 miles) to find food.

Smallest

Little penguins are the smallest members of the penguin family. They are the only ones that **breed** in Australia. Little penguins are half the size of most penguins – only 40 centimetres (12 inches) tall.

▲ Emperor penguins are the only ones that can **survive** the Antarctic winter.

Amazing bodies

Cold feet

Birds' feet do not seem to feel the cold, or heat. Their feet are mostly made of strong **tendons** covered in **scales**. They have few nerves and blood vessels to get damaged by ice or hot rocks.

Birds live in many different places, from forests and mountains to open plains and oceans. Their bodies have adapted to different places and different lifestyles.

Feet

Most birds have four toes. Many birds, such as parrots, have toes that will grip so they can sit in trees. **Waders** have long, thin toes for walking on the seashore. Swimming birds have skin joining their toes to make **webbed** feet. These act like paddles in the water.

▼ The curlew's long toes are good on soft, wet mud.

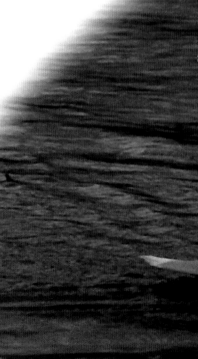

Wild words   wader bird that spends a lot of time walking in shallow water

Wings

Eagles and vultures have wide, long wings with large feathers at the end that look like fingers. These give the birds much more control when they fly high above the ground, **gliding** on warm currents of air.

The wandering albatross has long, thin wings. It can soar in the air over the ocean for many days without needing to land.

▼ The swan's webbed feet paddle below the water.

Life on the wing

The wandering albatross (above) spends most of its life flying. The bird can travel up to 14,500 kilometres (9,000 miles) in one flight. In just one day it can fly 885 kilometres (550 miles).

---

webbed having a thin skin joining the toes together

Breathing

All animals need **oxygen** to live. Birds take in oxygen in the air they breathe. Their lungs are linked to air pockets and hollow bones, which let air flow all around the body. The oxygen is carried in the bloodstream to the muscles.

Flying birds need very strong chest muscles to beat their wings and stay in the air. These muscles use a lot of oxygen. Flapping wings is hard work.

Flying dinosaurs

Fossils of dinosaurs that had wings have been found in China. These dinosaurs may have been the flying, or **gliding**, **ancestors** of birds.

oxygen one of the gases in air and water that all living things need

Birds' hearts have to work hard to pump enough oxygen-rich blood around the body when they are flying. **Flightless** birds have smaller hearts in relation to their size.

The tiny hummingbird has a large heart because it beats its wings 80 times a second. This helps it to hover in the air while it sips **nectar** from flowers.

Heart rate

The heart rate of the tiny, ruby-throated hummingbird is 615 beats per minute. That is nearly three times as fast as a chicken's heart rate – at about 245 beats per minute.

▲ Hummingbirds are able to hover to drink nectar from flowers.

nectar sugary fluid produced by flowers

Eyes

Birds have very good eyesight. Most birds have a wider view than we do. Owls have their eyes at the front of their head. This means they can see a wide area with both eyes at the same time. They need to focus on the same area with both eyes. Then they can judge how far away their **prey** is.

All-round vision

Ducks can see almost right around without moving their heads, so they can spot **predators** coming. This is because their eyes are on the sides of their heads.

▼ The great horned owl can turn its head right round without turning its body.

▲ The golden eagle can see its prey from high above the ground.

prey animal that is killed and eaten by other animals

Ears

A bird's ears are hidden inside its head. Long-eared and short-eared owls look as if they have ears on the top of their heads. These are just feathers.

Some birds have much better hearing than we do. They can hear very soft sounds. Barn owls can hunt small animals in the dark, using their sharp ears to find a mouse.

Sharp senses

The great horned owl is able to see 35 times further than most people. It can see a mouse moving at night from over a kilometre (half a mile) away.

▼ The eyes of an eagle owl are many times stronger than ours.

Feeding

Birds need to eat lots to keep them flying. Most birds have to eat at least half their own weight every day. That is a bit like a twelve-year-old boy eating about forty pizzas in one day.

Beaks

Birds do not have teeth and do not chew their food. They use their beaks to tear off bits or to crush food before they swallow it.

Power drill

The black woodpecker (right) has a very tough beak and a strong neck. To get at grubs under the bark, it hammers at trees with its beak, about 10,000 times a day.

Different beaks for different jobs

You can actually tell what kind of food a bird eats from the shape of its beak. Short, fat beaks are good for crushing seeds. Sharp, hooked beaks are better for ripping flesh. Long, thin beaks help **waders** to dig into sand and mud, looking for food.

There are 13 very similar **species** of finch on the Galapagos Islands. Thousands of years ago, they may all have had the same type of beaks. Gradually, over a very long period of time, their beaks changed to suit the different foods that they ate.

Tools of the trade

The woodpecker finch (below right) is found on the Galapagos Islands. It uses twigs or cactus spines as tools to dig out food.

▶ The common cactus finch lives on the Galapagos Islands.

23

Insect-eaters

Many small birds eat insects. They help to keep the numbers of insects down. A lot of birds also eat berries, nuts, and seeds.

Seed-eaters

Seed-eaters help young trees and other plants to grow in different places. Some seeds pass out in the birds' droppings. They are scattered a long way from the parent plants. The droppings act like **fertilizer,** helping the seeds to grow.

Fire seeds

Kirtland's warbler from Michigan, USA, needs forest fires to **survive**. It eats the seeds of the jack pine tree, which are released only after a forest fire.

▼ The sand grouse eats 5000–8000 seeds a day.

Feeding in a hurry

Birds that eat seeds have a **crop** in their throat. This is where they keep food if they are feeding in a hurry.

First, the seeds are soaked in juices in the crop. Next, seeds pass into the **gizzard**. Here they are ground up.

Eating sand

Some birds that feed on hard, dry seeds also eat sand and gravel. This goes into the gizzard and helps grind up the food.

Weight training

The little sedge warbler (below) doubles its weight by eating lots of insects just before it leaves Europe. It flies without stopping for four days to spend the winter in South Africa – a journey of 9,000 kilometres (6,000 miles).

---

crop pouch in a bird's throat for keeping food

Fish-eaters

Many birds find their food in water. Some dig in the mud for worms and other small animals. Some fly low over rivers or seashores with their beaks open under the water. When they find a fish they flip it up into the air so they can catch it.

The beaks of some fish-eaters have rough edges that look like teeth. These hold onto slippery fish.

Would you believe it?

The puffin has an extra bone in its jaw. It can move its beak but still keep a tight grip. This means it can hold a whole row of fish without the ones near the end falling out.

　bill jaws and beak of a bird

Divers

The brown pelican is famous for its dive. It flies high above the water, then dives deep down into it. It has a pouch attached to its lower **bill** and throat. The pouch can stretch to hold many fish.

Fishing tricks

The green heron, from North America, drops a feather or a fly on the water and waits for a fish to come and take it. It then spears the fish with its sharp beak.

◄ The fish eagle is strong. It can catch large fish.

The African fish eagle has good eyesight. It flies high above lakes and rivers until it sees its **prey**. Then it dives down and grabs the fish in its **talons**.

talon claw of a bird of prey

Using tools

The Egyptian vulture (below) likes to eat ostrich eggs. It uses a stone to crack the tough shell.

Meat-eaters

Birds that eat meat spend less time feeding than the hungry seed-eaters. A seed-eating bird will need to eat hundreds of seeds and that takes much longer. But the meat-eaters have to spend a long time hunting.

Over 300 bird **species** eat meat, but not all of them kill it themselves. Vultures, crows, and many others eat animals that are already dead. They fly high in the sky and can see a body from a long way away.

▶ The great grey owl can hear a mouse over 50 metres (165 feet) away.

species type of living animal or plant

Eyes like a hawk

Falcons, buzzards, and hawks have amazing eyes. They fly high above the ground, looking for food. When they see their **prey**, they dive really fast, usually killing it on the spot.

Night owls

Most of the 135 species of owls in the world hunt at night. Their huge eyes can see in nearly total darkness and they can hear every sound. They **glide** silently, taking their prey by surprise.

Coughing up

In **birds of prey**, the **gizzard** grinds up all the hair and bones from the prey. The ground-up paste is made into a **pellet** that the bird spits out. If it is swallowed, the sharp bones could damage the bird's insides.

◀ This red-footed falcon is coughing up a pellet.

gizzard part of a bird's stomach that grinds down food

Thieves

Some birds, such as jays, magpies, and gulls, will steal eggs from nests and eat other birds' chicks.

Snowy owls

Snowy owls like to live in the cold, northern Arctic. But every three or four years they fly south. They are even seen as far south as the state of Georgia in the United States.

The owls fly there whenever there are a lot of **lemmings** to eat. Once they have eaten most of the lemmings, hunting is hard. They fly north again.

▼ This snowy owl is about to eat its small prey.

lemming small rodent, like a hamster

Kings of the sky

There are eagles all over the world, except Antarctica. They are the strongest **birds of prey**, and can kill big animals such as deer. They hold the **prey** with their strong **talons**, and push their sharp back claw through the back of the skull. This kills their prey quickly.

The South American harpy eagle has legs as thick as a human wrist. It is very strong and can carry monkeys as heavy as itself.

Nature's cleaners

Vultures do a good job of clearing up. They eat dead and rotting animals.

▼The greater spotted eagle (left) from India has thick feathers on its legs.

bird of prey bird that catches live animals for food

Breeding

Male birds are often colourful, or have fancy feathers to attract a **mate**. Some have special **mating calls** or dances.

Look at me

When it is time to **breed**, male prairie chickens, from North America, get together to show off to the females. They raise the feathers on the top of their heads and fan out their tails as they dance about. They also make sounds by sucking air into the yellow pouches in their necks (shown below) and then forcing it out again.

Blue jays

To attract a mate, the male blue jay brings tasty food to the female. He then feeds her as if she were a chick.

mate partner of the opposite sex

Home sweet home

The male wren does not have fine feathers. This little brown bird tries a different trick to find a mate. He makes lots of nests and then asks a female to choose one. This is where she will lay her eggs.

The bowerbird of New Guinea builds a bower, or nest-like structure, to attract a mate. He fills it with pretty stones, shells, and petals. Then he parades in front of it and sings.

Ruffs

Ruffs (below) live in marshes in Northern Europe. To attract the females, each male has a different pattern of feathers. No two males look the same.

Many partners

The male red-winged blackbird may have up to fifteen female mates. These North American birds (below) all nest together.

Families

Mute swans and some other birds live all their lives with a single **mate**. They often return to the same place to nest each year.

Bringing up their young takes a lot of time during the first few weeks of life. Parents are kept busy finding food for the hungry chicks.

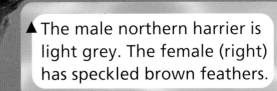

▲ The male northern harrier is light grey. The female (right) has speckled brown feathers.

Some birds have more than one partner. Harris hawks often live in groups of three, so there are three adults to feed the chicks.

The male northern harrier often mates with several females. This is most likely to happen if there is plenty of food and he does not need to help feed the young. The female (below) may also have more than one mate.

Three is company
Galapagos hawks (below) also live in threes. One female and two males share the job of bringing up the chicks.

Eggs

All birds lay eggs. Egg shells are very thin so the chick inside can breathe. They break easily, so the chick can peck through the shell to **hatch**.

Many birds lay eggs in a nest and sit on them to keep them warm and safe. Eggs are a good meal for many other animals, even some birds. The colours and patterns of eggs **camouflage** them, so **predators** are less likely to see them.

Extra large

The kiwi and the storm petrel both lay big eggs. The eggs weigh about a quarter of the bird's body weight.

▲ The storm petrel is a European seabird that nests in rocky places.

► A gull chick uses its **egg tooth** to hatch out of its shell.

hatch break out of the egg

Egg shapes

Many eggs are oval like chickens' eggs.
Owls and woodpeckers lay round eggs.
Guillemots lay their eggs on cliffs. The eggs
are long and thin with a point at one end.
They roll round in a circle if they are knocked,
so they do not fall off the cliff.

A good match

The Indian yellow
lapwing (above),
lays spotty eggs
that match the
soil or stones
around them.

Cuckoos

Cuckoos do not make their own nests. The female cuckoo lays just one egg in the nest of another bird.

When it **hatches** out of the egg, the cuckoo chick pushes all the other eggs and chicks out of the nest. The cuckoo's **foster parents** then have only one mouth to feed. The chick soon grows much bigger than the parents.

Safe nest

This blue tit has made a nest inside a hollow tree. Its chicks will be safe from **predators** and bad weather as they grow up.

▲ This cuckoo chick is pushing another egg out of the nest.

foster parents those who look after young in place of the natural parents

Chicks

Ducklings are born on the ground, so they have to be ready to walk right away. Chicks born in high nests often take longer to grow up. They may have no feathers and be blind at birth. They cannot fly until their feathers grow. They need their parents to bring food to them.

Learning to fly

When it is time to fly, some chicks just flutter a few feet to the ground. This young eagle (below) has to take off from a high cliff as it tries its wings.

Weird and wonderful

Messages

Many birds can make a number of different sounds to give messages to other birds. Songbirds may sound as though they are singing for joy, but song is mainly a way of talking with other birds. Some birds sing to say "This is my space – keep out!"

Birds have sounds for other messages too. You may have heard blackbirds making a loud 'tchink, tchink' sound to warn of a danger such as a cat in the garden.

Silent

The kestrel (below) is mostly silent. It makes sounds only when it is looking for a **mate**.

Man in court over rude mynah bird

A CHINESE MAN BECAME upset because his neighbour's mynah bird kept calling him rude names. When he went to court in Beijing in 2003, he played a recording of the bird, and everyone began to laugh.

Mimics

Starlings and thrushes are great **mimics**. Some have been heard copying telephone ring tones. The best mimic is probably the Indian mynah bird. It can 'talk' just like a person, although it probably does not understand the words.

Bird talk

Parrots and macaws can mimic words without knowing what they mean. However, Victor, a parakeet, learnt the sounds and meanings of over 1000 words. He could talk with his owner.

◄ This male indigo bunting sings loudly from a perch.

mimic (noun) one living thing that can copy another living thing

Travellers

Perhaps the most amazing skill of birds is their sense of direction. Some have super strength to **migrate** long distances. They know exactly where to fly.

Migrating birds fly thousands of kilometres. They can find the same place where they fed or nested before. In autumn you may see lots of swallows sitting on telephone wires. From Europe these birds migrate to Africa for the winter. They will return north to **breed** next summer.

Long-distance flier

The pectoral sandpiper migrates the furthest of any bird. It flies up to 19,000 kilometres (12,000 miles).

◄ The pectoral sandpiper migrates from North to South America.

migrate spend part of the year in one place and the rest of the year in another place

Clever crows

Crows in Japan have learned to use cars to crack walnuts, by dropping the nuts under the wheels.

Crows in California, in the United States, are now doing the same. They have learned that cars will stop when the traffic lights turn red. They dive down, with their nuts at the ready, even before the cars have stopped.

Gaggle of geese

Some birds often gather in groups like the ones below. Some of the names for groups are:

- Gaggle of geese
- Gulp of cormorants
- Murder of crows
- Parliament of owls
- Watch of nightingales
- Stand of flamingos.

▲ An Arctic tern sets off from the Arctic circle. It will fly 17,600 kilometres (11,000 miles) to Antarctica.

43

Hibernation

Birds often find it hard to find food during winter. The common poorwill gets through cold, North American winters by **hibernating**. It can survive 100 days on its body fat. This would only be enough to keep it alive for ten days if it was awake.

Extremes

Some birds live in freezing cold places. Others can **survive** the baking heat. Flamingos live in shallow lakes in Africa where the temperature can reach 60°C. They are not naturally pink. They change colour when they eat tiny shrimps that they catch in the hot lakes.

A flamingo lays just one white egg on a muddy mound. The egg is kept warm by the hot sun.

▶ Flamingos find shrimps in the shallow lake.

▼ Long, spreading toes help these coots to walk on ice.

hibernate the body closes down so the animal appears to be asleep during the winter

Freezing cold water

The giant coot, or ajoya, is a water bird. It lives in lakes in the snowy mountains of South America. In winter almost everything freezes so it cannot swim.

Hot springs

But there are some pools that are warmed by hot springs of water. The giant coots sit together in these pools until spring arrives.

Defence trick

The pitohui bird from Papua New Guinea has poison in its feathers and skin. Any small animal that eats it will die.

▲ This black-headed pitohui sings a warning that means 'Don't touch me!'

45

Smoky wings

Rooks have been seen standing on smoking chimneys with their wings open. They seem to like getting covered in smoke. Perhaps the smoke helps to kill insects.

Keeping clean

All birds **preen** to keep their feathers clean, but some birds call in the cleaners to help.

Over 250 bird **species** have been seen picking up ants and putting them on their bodies. The ants are thought to eat small insects living on the birds.

Cleaning others

Oxpeckers are liked by rhinos, buffaloes, giraffes, and zebras. These birds feed on insects and even ear wax. This helps to keep the animals clean.

▼ Is the oxpecker saying to the buffalo, "A word in your ear"?

preen tidy and oil the feathers

Happy to walk

The African secretary bird can fly, but likes to walk. It spends most of its time on the ground, and can walk as far as 32 kilometres (20 miles) a day.

The bird feeds on snakes, which it kills by stamping on them. It has thick, hard **scales** on its legs that protect it from bites. Secretary birds are so good at catching snakes, that farmers sometimes tame them. They keep snakes away from the farms.

Open wide

The little crocodile bird (above) steps into the mouth of the Nile crocodile in Egypt. It picks bits of meat from the crocodile's teeth.

◀ This secretary bird is about to kill a snake.

scales small, bony plates that protect the skin on fish, reptiles, and some birds

Birds in danger

In the last 400 years at least 115 **species** of bird have become **extinct**, and many are **endangered**.

Going ... going ...

The beautiful Bali starling became a popular pet. Many were caught and sold. There are thought to be only four left in the wild.

Gone

The American passenger pigeon was once so common that millions were trapped and shot as a pest. Unfortunately it became extinct. The last one died in Cincinnati Zoo in 1914.

Rarest bird

Macaws have been caught and sold as pets. In 2000 the last male Spix's blue macaw disappeared from the Brazilian rainforest where it lived.

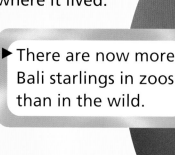

▶ There are now more Bali starlings in zoos than in the wild.

Making a comeback

The California condor, a huge vulture, was once common across North America. As towns sprang up and wild animals began to disappear, the numbers of condors fell dramatically.

To save these birds from dying out, the last wild condor was caught in 1987. Since then condors have been **bred** in zoos to release into the wild. In 2002, a condor chick **hatched** in the wild. This was the first wild-born condor for 20 years.

▼ There is hope for the Californian condor.

Billion-dollar bird

The Guanay cormorant of Peru is known as the "billion-dollar bird", because its droppings make good fertilizer. The droppings are taken from under the cliffs where the birds live.

Birds and us

Humans have always loved birds for their songs, their colours, and the way they fly. We also need birds. They are an essential part of the Earth's **ecology**.

- Birds eat insects that harm crops, and they also eat mosquitoes.
- Some birds, such as hummingbirds, help to **fertilize** plants.
- Seed-eaters spread seeds through their droppings, so new wildflowers and trees grow in different places.

ecology relationship between animals, plants, and the Earth

Under threat

Humans hurt birds in many ways. Birds' homes have been destroyed for farming and building. Finding food and nesting places is more difficult.

Fishermen have taken many fish from the sea. Seabirds find it harder to get food. **Pollution** in the sea affects fish. Seabirds can be poisoned by eating polluted fish.

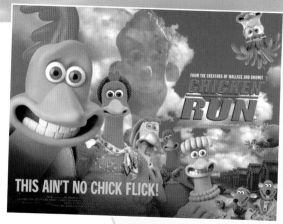

THIS AIN'T NO CHICK FLICK!

Bird survivors

In the cartoon film, *Chicken Run*, the humans treat the birds badly. The brave hens show that birds can **survive**. Will birds in the wild be as lucky?

◄ This penguin has been covered in oil that spilled from a damaged ship. It will not live.

pollution damage caused by chemicals, fumes, and rubbish

Find out more

Websites

BBC Wildfacts
Go to the 'Birds' group in the Advanced Search options. You will find photos and information on all sorts of birds.
www.bbc.co.uk/ nature/wildfacts

Bird Extremes
Go to 'Birds' in the Science/Biology section. Then click on 'Bird extremes'.
www.enchanted learning.com/ subjects

PBS Life of Birds
Lots of information and good photos on birds all round the world.
www.pbs.org/ lifeofbirds

Books

Classifying Living Things: Birds, Andrew Solway (Heinemann Library, 2003)
From Egg to Adult: The Life Cycle of Birds, Mike Unwin (Heinemann Library, 2003)
Eagles and Birds of Prey, Jemima Parry-Jones (Dorling Kindersley, 2000)

World wide web

To find out more about birds you can search the Internet. Use keywords like these:
- ostrich
- flightless +birds
- "peregrine falcon"

You can find your own keywords by using words from this book. The search tips below will help you find useful websites.

Search tips

There are billions of pages on the Internet. It can be difficult to find exactly what you are looking for. These tips will help you find useful websites more quickly:

- Know what you want to find out about
- Use simple keywords
- Use two to six keywords in a search
- Only use names of people, places, or things
- Put double quote marks around words that go together, for example "birds of prey"

Where to search

Search engine

A search engine looks through millions of website pages. It lists all the sites that match the words in the search box. You will find the best matches are at the top of the list, on the first page.

Search directory

A person instead of a computer has sorted a search directory. You can search by keyword or subject and browse through the different sites. It is like looking through books on a library shelf.

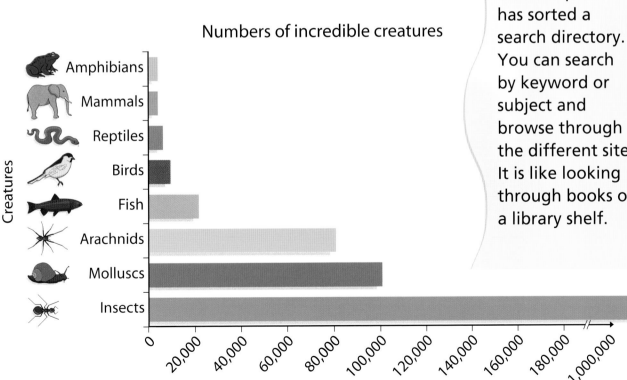

Numbers of incredible creatures

Glossary

ancestors relatives that lived a long time ago

bill jaws and beak of a bird

bird of prey bird that catches live animals for food

breed to produce young

camouflage colours and patterns that match the background

crop pouch in a bird's throat for keeping food

display behave in a way that will attract a mate

ecology relationship between animals, plants, and the Earth

egg tooth sharp spike on chick's beak for breaking out of the egg

endangered in danger of dying out

evolve change very slowly over time

extinct died out, never to return

fertilizer something that is put into the soil to help plants to grow

flightless unable to fly

fossil remains of a plant or animal that lived a very long time ago

foster parents those who look after young in the place of the natural parents

gizzard part of a bird's stomach that grinds down food

glide move smoothly without flapping wings

hatch break out of the egg

hemisphere the Earth is made of two halves, the Northern and Southern hemispheres

hibernate the body closes down so the animal appears to be asleep during the winter

lemming small rodent, like a hamster

mate partner of the opposite sex

mating male and female coming together to produce young

mating call special sound made by an animal to attract a mate

migrate spend part of the year in one place and the rest of the year in another place

mimic (noun) one living thing that can copy another living thing

moult lose feathers before growing new ones

nectar sugary fluid produced by flowers

oxygen one of the gases in air and water that all living things need

pellet bones and fur from prey squashed into a small cylinder. It is coughed up by birds of prey.

pollution damage caused by chemicals, fumes, and rubbish

predator animal that hunts and eats other animals

preen tidy and oil the feathers

prey animal that is killed and eaten by other animals

reptile cold-blooded animal with scales, such as a snake or lizard

rodent small mammal with sharp teeth such as mouse, squirrel, and rat

roost settle down to sleep

scales small, bony plates that protect the skin on fish, reptiles, and some birds

settlers people who move to live in a new country

species type of living animal or plant

survive stay alive despite danger and difficulties

talon claw of a bird of prey

tendon strand of strong tissue that joins muscle to bone

wader bird that spends a lot of time walking in shallow water

waterproof does not let in water

webbed having a thin skin joining the toes together

wingspan distance from one wing tip to the other when both wings are fully stretched

Index

Titles in the *Freestyle Express*: *Incredible Creatures* series include:

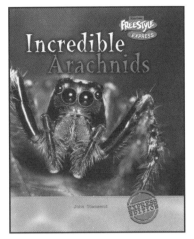

Hardback: 1844 434516

Hardback: 1844 434524

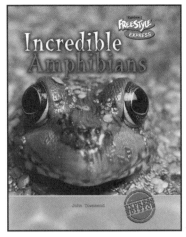

Hardback: 1844 434532

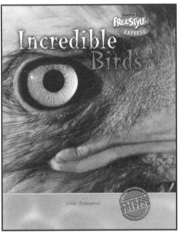

Hardback: 1844 434540

Hardback: 1844 434761

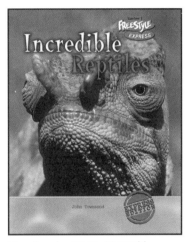

Hardback: 1844 43477X

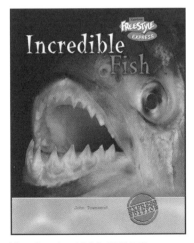

Hardback: 1844 435172

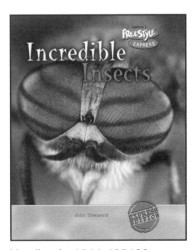

Hardback: 1844 435180

Find out about other Freestyle Express titles on our website www.raintreepublishers.co.uk